don't you need some Rest?

52 sabbath Reflections for stressful Living

Don't You Need Some Rest?

52 Sabbath Reflections for Stressful Living

Susie M. Paige

A Division of WINEPRESS PUBLISHING

Pleasant Word (a division of WinePress Publishing, PO Box 428, Enumclaw, WA 98022) functions only as book publisher. As such, the ultimate design, content, editorial accuracy, and views expressed or implied in this work are those of the author.

All Scripture references marked KJV are taken from the King James Version of the Bible.

ISBN 1-4141-0495-2
Library of Congress Catalog Card Number: 2005904593

Dedication

Dedicated to
Mom and Daddy
with thanks for teaching me
the value of work and rest.

table of contents

America does not readily sit still, even for a day.
—Alexis McCrossen

Historian and author of *Holy Day, Holiday: The American Sunday*

Introduction
why sabbath stories?

Dear Reader:

I am a baby boomer born in the 1950s, and society changed in many ways as I came of age. While my nieces and nephews never knew a time when society regarded any one day of the week differently than the others, I remember the Saturday shutdown of stores in Jewish communities and the Sunday closings of virtually all businesses in my neighborhood. I also recall not playing records (compact discs weren't on the market yet) or cards on Sunday because it was Sunday. After Sunday school and church service, my family had a special dinner. Sometimes we would go on drives in the country. There was little concern about the cost of gasoline then. In the summer, my dad would pile my sisters, girlfriends, and me into our family station wagon and take us all out for soft ice cream. We didn't get just ice cream cones. It was Sunday, and he would buy us any frozen treat we wanted, including the most expensive item on the dessert menu and my favorite, a banana split. So, from as far back as I can remember, Sunday felt different in my spirit, and I liked that.

Don't You Need Some Rest?

Like many of my generation and those that came before me, I was taught to live by the Ten Commandments. Honor God, use his name reverently, honor parents, don't steal, lie, kill, commit adultery, or be jealous summarizes nine of the holy laws. I believe I am a better person when I live by those principles. Then there is the fourth commandment to remember the Sabbath Day and keep it holy. Is it obsolete for me and our time, or even more necessary? While leisure activities appear to be at an all-time high, rest (the meaning of Sabbath) doesn't seem to abound.

As I sought ways to apply Commandment Four in my adult life, I began talking with others and exploring Sabbath thoughts, memories, and practices. I discovered I was not alone in wanting to know what Sabbath means in a practical way today, even by those that called it by a different name. Essayist Anne Taylor Fleming did a commentary on findings from doctors at Northwestern University that reported a connection between the pace at which families live and children's health. Researchers didn't recommend people practice Sabbath traditions when they released a study showing that a driven lifestyle can lead children to have hypertension and heart trouble later in life, but they did warn what happens to youngsters when they don't slow down.

Alvin Rosenfeld, MD and Nichole Wise authored the book, *The Overscheduled Child*, to help parents avoid the pressure to feel that the more activities and lessons children have, the better they will be able to compete as adults. Producer John de Graaf became so concerned about an epidemic of overwork and over-scheduling that he co-authored the book *Affluenza*, made a PBS documentary of the same name, and organized *Take Back Your Time Day*. It seems we need some rest.

The stories and quotes gathered here are a testimony that these contemporary professionals are right. The direction they are pointing us to is as old as time. You will hear it in the recollections that follow.

Introduction: Why Sabbath Stories?

Allow them to help you seek, find, or continue having Sabbath in your life. At the end, there is an opportunity for you to share your Sabbath stories and keep a journal. God's mandated gift of divine rest is a never-ending present that sits and waits to be unwrapped. It's yours to accept or leave unopened. Thank you for reading.

—Susie M. Paige

1

sabbath defined

Sabbath\Sab'bath': from the Hebrew noun *shabbath,* meaning to rest from labor. *(American Heritage Dictionary of the English Language)*

2

The spice that money can't buy—A folktale

A Roman emperor once visited the house of very poor Jewish family. To his surprise he found them laughing and singing, as if they were at a feast, even though there was not much food on the table. The Jews invited the emperor to join them, and soon he was eating some of the most delicious food he had ever tasted.

When he returned to the palace, the emperor summoned his cooks and described what he had eaten. He ordered them to prepare a similar meal, but try as they might, it never tasted the same as the food he had eaten in that poverty-stricken house.

Eventually, in desperation, he sent for the head of the Jewish family and asked what was in the food that he had missed out. "There is an ingredient with all your wealth you cannot buy," replied the Jew. "It is the finest spice there is. When it is added, even a snack is a banquet."

"Tell me what it is, and I shall buy it," ordered the emperor.

"I'm afraid not," answered the Jew. "It's called *Shabbat*."

3
Exodus 20:8

Remember the sabbath day, to keep it holy.

4

Remember the Sabbath

When I was a parish minister, responsible for the community of people under my jurisdiction, there was no hope of remembering the Sabbath, at least in the Hebrew sense of resting from my labors. If I wanted a Sabbath, I had to make it a moveable feast. Often it was a Friday or a Monday, when I turned off the ringer on my telephones and spent the day in solitary pursuits. It remained a workday, however. I did laundry. I wrote sermons. I balanced the checkbook. As much as I craved a true Sabbath, I did not believe I could afford one. If I did nothing for one day, then there would be twice as much in the next day.

When I left parish ministry, Sundays were free and clear. There was no reason in the world why I could not observe Sabbath—except for the compulsion of mine to produce, perform, and accomplish. I continued to work seven days a week until Lent 2000, when I decided to obey the fourth commandment. One day a week, I could lie back in God's arms. One day a week, whether or not my work was done, I would live as if I was free.

Remember the Sabbath

The Torah is very straightforward: "you shall not do any work." The key for me was freedom from compulsion. One day a week, the words "should," "ought," and "must" had no power over me. On Sundays I did not worship the clock, the dollar, or my superego. I worshipped God instead, whom I trusted to run the world for one day without my help. I cannot even bring myself to tell you how I spent those days, since my mind still calls it sloth.

It was not sloth. It was Sabbath, and its effect was immediate. Relationships became more spacious. Time itself became more spacious. Instead of charging out of the gate on Monday mornings, I found myself sauntering instead, still relishing the freedom of the day before. There was never enough time to get everything done, but I finally understood there never would be. There would only be enough time to live, with as much gratitude as I could muster.

Sabbath remains. My hold on it feels so tenuous. I am so tempted to go to the workshop of other gods, whose first requirement of me is that I relinquish my holy freedom. Week by week, I keep reaching for the gift God has offered me—the one human beings are so reluctant to accept that God made it a commandment.

Once when I attended a funeral at an African American Baptist church, the preacher consoled us by telling us that the person we loved had gone on to that place where everyday is Sunday. At the time, I believe I flinched. Now I know what he meant. We do not have to wait until we die to experience resurrection. God is ready whenever we are, with a weekly rehearsal for those who are willing to lie back in His arms.

—Barbara Brown Taylor
Author of *When God Is Silent*
Preprinted with permission from the
Lord's Day Alliance of Pennsylvania
www.sundayschoolhelp.com/alliance.htm

5

sabbath reflection

Sabbath emphasizes holiness and social justice.
Slaves cannot take a day off; free people can.
—Dorothy C. Bass
Author of *Practicing Our Faith*

6

The Joy of 24/6

In college, I lived downstairs from an Orthodox Jewish girl who, on Friday evenings, would disappear from the regular flow of campus life to observe the Sabbath. I asked her once how she felt about missing out on the things that preoccupied the rest of us, particularly the parties that I found so compelling. She told me simply she was grateful for the rest.

I am not a religious person. And I don't mean to trivialize my former neighbor's religious observances (which I know were far richer than she let on). But almost twenty years later I find that I have become a Sabbath observer of sorts, too. And I, too, am grateful for the rest. Let me explain.

My observance began during a time when I was working at home, alone, and going out with friends nearly every night and most weekends. I was expending enormous energy on both my work and my social life, but neither was satisfying. In fact, behind my game exterior I felt the beginnings of depression increasingly left me lying on my bed waiting for clues to emerge from within me as to how it

21

could be healed. The best time for this, of course, was on Sunday afternoons, when there was relatively little else to do.

But even Sunday had its distractions—brunches, movies, dinner parties. At first, I began cutting back on these selectively, maybe go to dinner, but skip the movie. Eventually, I began avoiding any and all social obligations that required me to leave home that day. When pressed for an explanation, I would jokingly tell those whose invitations I was declining that I was observing "a personal Sabbath." Surprisingly, few balked at the excuse, and as the habit stuck, so did the term.

One can only lie around for so long, however. After a while, my passive introspection gave way to homebound activities that, with practice, acquired the quality of ritual. In the empty space my Sabbath created, cleaning became a cathartic process that I now actually enjoy. Once a month, I'll go so far as to roll up the carpets and mop the floors. Sometimes I even do windows.

Cooking, another task I avoided, has also become a Sabbath fixture. In the fall and winter, when the days are short, I spend much of the afternoon preparing elaborate (for me) dishes, like chicken soup or lasagna. I eat these home-cooked suppers early and slowly, looking out over the backyard from my dining table as light from the setting sun streams in through the (clean!) windows.

The summer my landlord gave me permission to plant a garden, Sundays became a day for doing big outdoor tasks such as turning the soil, planting tomatoes inside their cages, or building trestles for snow peas. Another Sunday ritual is a long walk with my dog, an aging collie mix named Emma. We live too far from the nearest park for her to walk there and back, but I've discovered that Sunday morning, when other passengers are scarce, is one time when taxis will give us a ride.

Observing my Sabbath may mean making no plans with others, but it doesn't mean being entirely alone. While working in the garden, for example, I got to know my neighbors, a friendly couple who provided much-appreciated advice and encouragement across the chain-link fence that separates our yards. Sometimes, returning from the park, Emma and I will stop by the home of a couple I rarely see anymore, as they are preoccupied by the raising of two small children. The kids will let us in and we will play with their favorite new toys—or with Emma—until Mom or Dad wakes. Then, after a cup of coffee and some more conversation, Emma and I will be on our way. Everything I do on my Sabbath is informed by the singular condition of having large pools of time in which to do it. Nothing is rushed. Nothing is taken for granted. Everything fills its own space. And whatever doesn't get completed becomes, de facto, unimportant. Take magazines, for example. In the past, those that went unread accumulated into a reproachful stack. Now, whatever I do not read by Sunday night goes out with the next day's recycling. If last week's *New Yorker Magazine* hasn't caught my attention by the end of my Sabbath, it's unlikely to do so.

Every couple of months, I will break my Sabbath by going away for the weekend or attending a birthday party for a longtime friend, but these forays always reinforce my commitment. However pleasurable they may be, they usually leave me feeling slightly disoriented. My week has lost its rhythm, my apartment is a mess, or I'm tired and feeling disconnected from myself.

Over time, I have come to see the utilitarian value of my personal Sabbath. It's a good thing to be well rested, well fed, and well organized. But, much to my surprise, I've come to recognize deeper components as well. On a simple level, I find that my Sabbath puts me in a better frame of mind to appreciate the remainder of my week. These days, in contrast with two years ago when I began this practice, I often find myself feeling gratitude for my work and my social life. And gratitude, as I see it, is quintessentially spiritual. I also find spiritual comfort in the creation story, upon which the traditional Sabbath is based, that the world was created in six days, with the seventh set aside for rest. I find similar comfort in the commandments given to Moses in the Book of Exodus, "Remember the sabbath day, to keep it holy." For in both passages I recognize a connection between my Sabbath experience and centuries of observance by Jews and Christians. Even if the details of our observance differ, this connection lifts my experience from the personal to the universal. It connects me to other people like my neighbor from college. I wish I could recall the exact conversation I had with her all those years ago, because it occurs to me now that if she had said precisely, "I am grateful for the rest," she might have been playing a pun, meaning either that she was grateful for the opportunity to rest, or grateful for the rest of the week, or perhaps grateful for the community she shared as a result of her Sabbath. Of course, there's no point in speculating about someone else's feelings when I can speak of my own. When I say, "I am grateful for the rest," I mean it all three ways.

—Robin Campbell
Freelance writer
Used by permission of *Spirituality and Health Magazine*
www.spiritualityhealth.com

7

sabbath saying

Some days you should stop and rest. Wait for your soul to catch up with your body.

—African Sabbath saying

8

sunday shoes

My sisters and I always sat by the kitchen stove and got our hair pressed with a straightening comb on Saturday. My aunt was a beautician and she gave us curls. We couldn't comb them out until Sunday. I know my friends had to take their Sunday clothes and Sunday shoes off when they got home after church, but my grandmother took that ritual one step further. After we got undressed, she locked our outfits in the closet so we wouldn't be tempted to wear them before the next week. The best was saved for Sunday—clothes and food. It was about wearing your best for God and thanking Him over the best meal. I've kept up a Sunday dinner tradition. You might find ham or baked turkey on my table anytime, not just on holidays. I never wash clothes or shop on Sunday. Thinking back, even when my children were young, we didn't do a lot on Sunday. Mostly, we stayed home unless something special was happening. The day was filled with time at church—morning service, afternoon Sunday school, and BTU* (Baptist Training Union). It was a time to worship God together. After that, we'd settle in and just be with one another.

—Mary Sawyer
Church office staff member

*Baptist Training Union (BTU) are classes usually held Sunday afternoon where adults and children have denominational study, Bible drills, discussion of contemporary issues, and learn about other faiths. It's also called Baptist Youth Prayer Union (BYPU).

9

ɛzɛkiel 20:12

Moreover also I gave them my Sabbaths, to be a sign between me and them, that they might know that I am the Lord that sanctify them.

10

prized possession

Everyone I knew growing up looked forward to Sunday. I liked it because it was the time to get dressed up and be with my friends, wearing something other than school or play clothes. Among my crowd, a Sunday suit was a prized possession. Just about all the men and boys had one—navy blue or black with a matching tie. Men's apparel was limited in color then so all shirts were white. I didn't realize it as a child, but the adults around us used the clothing and food to mark Sunday as a special day of rest and worship. It gave our community the opportunity to come together and share in the blessings of God. The Sabbath was made for all people for our good. It's a divine present I never turn down.

—James E. Paige, Sr.
Bible teacher

11
sabbath Reflection

The Sabbath cannot strive in exile,
a lone stranger among days of profanity.
—Abraham Joshua Heschel
Jewish scholar

12

HOME RULE

My husband had a rule in our house. On Sunday, up until they were age sixteen, the children had to go to church. After that, it was their choice. He didn't always go like he should have, but he sent them. When I was growing up, my mama put down rolls every Saturday night and cooked them Sunday morning. The last time I tried to do that, the yeast went wild, and I had dough everywhere.

To socialize on Sunday, my family would go to the park, visit relatives and friends, or ride the double-decker bus through the city. Sometime we'd go downtown and window-shop. Jewish stores in our neighborhood would be closed on Saturday and open for a little while on Sunday. Now everything is open on Sunday. That's still surprising to me.

The older I get, the more I'm learning what it means to honor the Sabbath, to observe the Lord's Day. I used to think some of my parents' Sunday traditions didn't have any merit. Yet today, I don't wash clothes nor do any chores on Sunday. One day soon I'm going to have to try and find some of that salt mackerel my mother used to cook on Sundays. I might even try to bake those rolls again. As a child, I didn't know I was poor until somebody told me. There wasn't much money, but in many ways those were rich years. It may have been because of the way we started each week—what we did and didn't do on Sunday.

—Ruth Ludrick
Senior citizen Sunday school student

13

sabbath reflection

<blockquote>
The soul withers without the Sabbath.
(Easton's 1897 Bible Dictionary)
</blockquote>

14

NOT FOR ALL THE TEA IN CHINA

A kindly gesture from a church member allowed Mike and Hilary Mallett of Norwich, England to expand their business, *The Tea Junction*, from a wall kiosk to larger space in the Castle Mall. They signed a ten-year lease to be open during "core business hours" established by the mall tenant's association. The Mallets were dismayed when the association "moved the goalpost" by first voting to open for ten pre-Christmas Sundays in the mid-90s and then by extending this to permanent Sunday openings in 1999. Today, with one or two exceptions, most of the shops in the mall open every Sunday, but Mike and Hilary's *Tea Junction* was the first to do so.

"Against our better judgment, we initially abided by the first ten-week pre-Christmas opening, knowing the Bible's teaching on this issue," explains Mike. "And each year, after Christmas, I suffered mysterious illnesses and regularly found myself having to take time off to recuperate in January." But when Sunday opening became the norm last year, Mike and Hilary realized that the loss of church fellowship and teaching would become a permanent feature for them and staff members. They decided to make a stand. "This year we did not even open on Sundays over Christmas," reports Mike, "and for the first time in years I have not had post-Christmas illness as in other years. We undoubtedly lost some money over that period, but, perversely, we have already made up much of that loss with higher than usual sales figures for January. We do believe God is honoring us in our stand."

The odds are heavily weighted against Christian traders in high-profile city malls like Norwich, however. "When it comes to voting on the Sunday trading issue," explains Mike, "the number of votes given to individual traders depends on the size of their business." When it came to voting on changes to the terms of traders' leases, *The Tea Junction* held only one vote. "We did not stand much of a chance. But the fact remains that, although we cannot force our beliefs on others, neither can they force their beliefs on us. If we were a Muslim company and we were talking about closing for Friday prayers, they would not dare to create a fuss. Somehow, with Christians it is different."

Mike is very clear that *The Tea Junction* is not just about selling tea and coffee. He and Hilary believe God wants them there and that the current debate is one they are called to "walk in" rather than merely "get through." The Malletts have continued to resist ongoing pressure from the tenants association to open on Sunday. Their stand has led to local media coverage and has won them the support of Christians and non-Christians alike. "Customer after customer has read the sign we have placed on the doors stating our reasons for not opening on Sunday," says Mike. One lady even sought him out one Monday to tell him, "I am not a believer, but I just want you to understand that I admire your stand. I tried your doors yesterday [Sunday], and I just wanted you to know that I am back today."

The chairman of the Castle Mall Tenant Association, and manager of another mall store, told the local newspaper, "We are not saying he [Mike] or his family has to work on Sunday. The agreement says his unit should trade." However, the chairman of the tenants association appears to be oblivious that this is not an argument that cuts any ice with the fourth commandment. Mike already told the association that while they employ both Christians and non-Christians, they will not ask anyone else to work on Sunday in their stead. Sadly, too many today are hugely ignorant of the fact that the fourth commandment requires not only that, "In it [the Sabbath], you should do no work," but also: "nor your son, nor your daughter, nor your manservant, nor your maid servant, nor your cattle, nor your stranger who is within your gates." In short, the fourth commandment rules out not only our own Sunday working but also our allowing anyone else, either a worker or a guest, to work so long, as they are "under our roof." In this way, the application of the commandment not only constrains us privately but also sends out a powerful public message to society as a whole. An extremely healthy and beaming Mike says, "My wife, Hilary, got there ahead of me on this issue. It took me a while to realize that God knew better than me. I had become weighed down physically, mentally, and spiritually with the practicalities of coping with the dilemma. I missed the fellowship and felt like a stranger in my own church. But, I am very happy to say, that's all changed now." *The Tea Junction* buys its stock from Christian merchants who buy from independent organic farmers where possible. In this way, the business has been able to retain a strong fair trade policy. If you are in Norwich, do go and see Mike and Hilary in their super second floor shop. Just don't call on them on Sunday.

—Reprinted by permission of the
Lord's Day Observance Society
Day One Magazine
www.lordsday.co.uk

15
sabbath reflection

Some people claim we lose 20 percent of our sales by being closed on Sunday, but I know the Lord has honored me and this company for the decision to stay closed. Whether they are Christians or not, people appreciate it when you stick to your convictions.

—Truett Cathy
Founder and Chairman of Chick-fil-A
*(Over 800 of Mr. Cathy's fast food
restaurants are found across America.
Since inception of the company in 1946,
all operations have been closed on Sundays.)*

16

Take Back Your Time Day october 24

Americans are working too much, according to eighty-five percent of the 7800 those that participated in a CNN money.com poll. Four in five Americans wish they had more time to spend with family, according to a poll commissioned by the Center for a New American Dream, and half of all Americans even say they'd trade some of their pay for more time off.

Their concerns are buttressed by the fact that barely half of all Americans took a week's vacation in the summer of 2002 and that while millions of Americans have lost their jobs to the recession, many more are working longer hours and more mandatory overtime than ever.

"The evidence is clear—over-work and over-scheduling are pressing, daily concerns for many Americans," says John de Graaf, national coordinator for "Take Back Your Time Day" and editor of the book, *Take Back Your Time.* "We want people to know that the problem is not theirs alone, it is a national concern that needs to be addressed now."

Take Back Your Time Day

October 24 is "Take Back Your Time Day," a non-partisan educational initiative to address the problems of over-work, over-scheduling, and what the organizers are calling "time poverty." October 24 falls nine weeks before the end of the year, symbolizing the nine weeks—350 hours—more each year that Americans work compared to western Europeans.

From Anchorage, Alaska to Boston, Massachusetts and from Washington D.C. to San Diego, thousands of Americans gather at community centers, places of worship, union halls, museums, bookstores, and on university and college campuses for a national conversation about how Americans can live more balanced lives.

"The interest we've received has been very encouraging. It's crossed economic, political and cultural lines," says Gretchen Burger, lead organizer of "Take Back Your Time Day." The campaign has won endorsements from labor unions, religious and family organizations, and politicians. A US Senate resolution was passed unanimously declaring October National Work and Family Month, with the goal of "reducing the conflict between work and family." Mayors of Seattle, Washington, and Duluth, Minnesota and the governor of Michigan were among the first elected officials across the nation to officially proclaim October 24 "Take Back Your Time Day" in their jurisdictions.

"'Take Back Your Time Day'" is not anti-work," says Jeanette Watkins, founder of People for a Shorter Work Week and "Take Back Your Time Day" volunteer. "But American life has gotten way out of balance. Americans are working harder than ever as they are forced to sacrifice the things that really matter like good health, active citizenship and time for their families, nature and the soul. We need to bring the balance back."

"Take Back Your Time Day" is a project of the Center for Religion, Ethics and Social Policy at Cornell University and is the first national initiative of the Simplicity Forum. Learn more at www.timeday.org.

17

wonderful rest

Preparation for Sunday in our house began Saturday evening. Mother made light rolls. I always had little doll-size ones she'd let me knead on the side. They were set aside to rise overnight. Chickens were rung on Saturday too. I had nine brothers and sisters, and we lived in a country town in Virginia. The Saturday night bath everyone received was quite a ritual. One by one, starting with the youngest, we each took a bath in a tin tub behind our old pot-bellied stove in the kitchen, the warmest room in the house. My girlfriend's father used to tell her and her siblings to "bathe up as far as possible, bathe down as far as possible, then you bathe possible." I adopted his pattern for getting clean.

When the church bell rang that meant it was time to go to Sunday school. Our lessons were on small notepads, and we worked on little sheets. Everyone read Bible verses, and we always had pennies to put in the offering plate. Each year the church had a Sunday homecoming and families would save their prized hams and preserves for that celebration. Extended family and friends would visit. But we didn't have to wait until homecoming to eat well. There was always special food on Sunday. The light rolls made on Saturday were cooked for Sunday morning breakfast. The entire town smelled like fresh bread on Sunday morning. The chicken was cooked later, and there was always some special dessert, like lemon meringue pie.

Work was harder in those days, and we recycled before we knew the word. Ashes were saved to put on icy sidewalks so folks wouldn't fall in the winter. Old wool clothes were used to stuff quilts. Slop was fed to hogs. Cooking grease was made into soap. Children and adults worked all the time, but we always had Sunday to look forward to. The rest was wonderful.

—Erva M. Saunders
Retired elementary school speech teacher

18
Exodus 20:11

For in six days the Lord made heaven and earth, the sea, and all that in them is, and rested on the seventh day: wherefore the LORD blessed the sabbath day, and hallowed it.

19

Evening Dance

Sunday morning we always got up early. My mother made sure we had a hot breakfast—eggs, grits, bacon, toast, juice—the whole works. She would sit down with my brother, my sisters, and me, and we would all eat together. She always asked us if we knew what day it was. I think that was her way of reminding us that Sunday was something special to her and for us.

We always went to morning church service and afternoon Sunday school. We had to sit on the same pew our mother sat on until we were about sixteen years old. The only time we didn't have to sit with her was when the Sunday school choir or the junior choir sang. I sang with both groups. The Sunday school choir was seated on the far right hand side of the sanctuary. All of us children were always peeping to see our mothers. We'd wave at them throughout the service, getting their attention as if they didn't know we were there. As I got older, I sang in the junior choir but enjoyed being on the junior usher board best. We had an adult leader who was very strict but nice. He knew how to talk to young people. He'd always check our uniforms and check to see that we did everything correctly. I liked that. Folks who say children don't want discipline I disagree with. To this day, I try to do everything decently and in order. Being an usher helped teach me that.

On Sunday evenings, I always wanted to go to teen dances. There was a ballroom on the corner not far from our house, and youth dances were held Sundays around 6 P.M. My mother would never let us go. When we'd ask her why, she'd just say it was the Lord's Day—a day of rest. We had to sit on the porch. She'd tolerate a little noise during the week but not on Sunday. After a few warnings, if we didn't quiet down, we had to go into the house.

The one time she gave in and said we could go to the weekly dance, there was some kind of riot or fight in the place. Police and police dogs were everywhere, so we never got in. So that was the end of that. I eventually learned a few dance steps but not from any practice I got on Sunday night.

Nowadays on Sunday, I continue to get up early and say my prayers. Sometimes I cook before I leave the house. I still go to Sunday school. A lot of people may think it's only for children, but when I was a child I would read and study because I was told to. Now I read and study with conviction and understanding. Growing up, when it came to learning about women in the Bible, I only remember Mary, Sarah, and Delilah. Sunday school has prompted me to read and study on my own. I now know about many women in the Bible, the good girls and the bad girls. Knowing Bible stories is great, but applying them to my life now is even better.

For me, Sunday is still a day of rest and a time to renew my strength. I love to be quiet and reflect on what God has done for me the past week and what He wants me to know and do for the next. I go through the Sunday paper cover to cover, reviewing the news from the week, taking in the feature articles, and, of course, looking to see what is on sale, and clipping coupons. It doesn't matter if it takes me all afternoon and paper is all over my bedroom when I'm done. I'm in no hurry. With the markets, malls, and even banks open seven days a week and work shifts around the clock, people have to work at carving out some quiet time for worship and reflection. It's refreshing and worth the effort.

—Dianne N. Johnson
Hospital food services technician

20

sunday defined

Ancient Greeks and Romans, realizing the sun was the source of life on the planet, gave it prime importance in their thinking by naming the first day of the week *dies solis*, day of the sun.

The first day of the week since ancient times has been designated as the day of rest. The holy day of the week for Christians, also known as the Lord's Day, is based on the biblical account that Jesus Christ rose from the dead on the first day of the week (www.indepthinfo.com).

21

A Calming Experience

On Sunday I would awaken to the sound of my mother's voice saying, "Lisa, get up now so you won't be late for Sunday school." That was usually followed by, "I ran a little bath water for you. Come on and get in the tub before your water gets cold." As my mom opened the door to my bedroom, I'd smell the aroma of breakfast cooking. Getting us (my younger sister and me) up, bathed, and dressed was usually Mom's responsibility, and getting breakfast on the table was usually Daddy's duty. Sometimes there'd be a reversal, but not often.

By the time I got downstairs, there'd be a plate of hot food on the table (sometimes grits, sometimes home fries,) and Daddy would ask, "How do you want your eggs?" He always made eggs to order. My dad was an excellent cook. Sometimes there'd be fried fish, or creamed beef, or my personal favorite, smothered chicken. Daddy would always tell some tall tale about Mom having absolutely no cooking skills whatsoever until she married him. That always led to stories of how he taught her everything she knows. When the eggs were done, Daddy would cover me with his apron (I was a pretty sloppy eater), and we'd sit down to breakfast.

When we were done eating, Mom would comb my hair, and soon Deacon Jackson (my Sunday school teacher and the superintendent of our Sunday school) would honk the horn of his small yellow car, and off we went. His car was a Toyota of some sort. I don't remember the model. I do remember that it was a small car, and he packed what seemed like a million kids into it every Sunday. We loved it.

In retrospect, I can recall that Sister Jackson would ring the phone every Sunday morning to find out if my sister and I were going to Sunday school. Apparently, that was her responsibility in their family. She would call the home of every child on his route, and that was pretty much when everyone's Sunday morning began. I lived closest to the church, so I was last to be picked up. Sunday school started at 9:45. Deacon Jackson usually got to my house at 9:20. We'd be at the church by 9:30, and we'd laugh and talk until time to begin. It was never hurried. It was always a very calming experience.

Unfortunately, now on Sundays, I seem to be sleeping too far into the morning, awakening in a panic, and rushing to get myself to church. I have no idea when this downward spiral began. It was no doubt when my parents stopped getting me ready for church. I really hate that I am hurried every Sunday morning. My mother hates it as well (my dad is deceased), and she voices her disapproval quite often. My mother is the musician at the church I attended while growing up. She has been for over 30 years. She is never late for church. She is never hurried on Sunday morning. I marvel at that. My mother has a very solid sense of church etiquette, and lateness or rushing is totally unacceptable. I'm working on it.

I recently purchased a house and have begun creating a self-contained sense of home and family. I've also resolved to begin my Sundays with a calm focus. Already I strive to remember the Sabbath by aligning my career, my social life, my intellect, and my spirit life.

A Calming Experience

That honors God and others. It gives me Sabbath every day, because I have rest in my soul.

—Lisa Jane Erwin
Social worker

<h1 style="text-align:center">22</h1>

sundae defined

Sundae: A dish of ice cream with a topping, including syrup, fruit, nuts, or whipped cream. Evanston, Illinois passed a town ordinance in the 1800s prohibiting the selling of ice cream sodas on Sunday. Ingenious confectioners came up with the soda-less soda, or Sunday soda. Objections were made to naming the ice cream and syrup with no soda after the Sabbath so the spelling was changed. Ithaca, New York also claims to be the place where the sundae was created. (www.evanston.lib.il.us)

23

Dad's Day in the Kitchen

For the first eighteen years of my life, nearly every Sunday I woke to the smell of my father's cooking. My mother was the main cook Monday through Saturday, but on Sunday it was Dad's time in the kitchen. Although he would make us breakfast, the predominant smells were of beef or pork being prepared for Sunday night dinner. My father was of Italian dissent and loved to use seasonings and sauces. The aroma permeated the air up into my second-floor bedroom.

Sunday morning was spent eating and greeting family friends. They would stop by to visit, have a cup of coffee, and then we'd watch a parade of visitors come and go each and every week through the house. Mr. Mills, a bank branch manager, would come by early in the day, often before I was even up. He nearly became my alarm clock. "What's up, Dad?" (He called my father "Dad"). You could count on that like clockwork. My father would say, "Just coogin'" (not "cookin'" but "coogin'"). How about you?" Then came the classic line that is forever burned into my memory since I have been fourteen years old.

Don't You Need Some Rest?

Mr. Mills' response was always, "Just paintin' the house." My siblings and I have laughed for years that Mr. Mills was in a never-ending state of "painting the house." We wondered if it ever got finished. Today we still laugh and throw that line around when we are together. The *Murphy Brown* television show had a character that was unendingly painting her house. That to me was our Mr. Mills.

By noon, we children went to mass at the neighborhood Catholic church, which also ran the school we attended during the week. In the years before I started school, I recall my mom would dress in black and wear a hat or veils. We walked to church with her. My brothers and I would be dressed in pressed shirts and pants. Of course, my sister wore a dress.

My brothers and I were altar boys. In many ways that responsibility kept us going to church. I was rarely given a Sunday service. I was constantly used as a weekday altar boy. The Sunday services always used older more experienced altar boys, more my brothers' ages. Looking back, I remember feeling almost scared to serve on Sunday, because it meant you had to be good, on time, and had a large congregation in front of you. There was no time to make mistakes for all of your peers to see. That service gave me a lot of training in how to conduct myself in front of people. I got to know many of the church members over time.

I now live sixty miles from where I grew up and attend a Catholic church that looks like the one of my youth. Even the pastors resemble each other. I go to the same 12:15 P.M. mass each Sunday as I did as a youngster. I'm no longer an altar boy, obviously, and am amazed at how young and little the children look to me. I'm not that old! Now young girls are allowed to serve mass, which wasn't done during my childhood.

After mass I sometimes go with a friend to have coffee. Most of my family gatherings still tend to be on a Sunday, so I often drive to visit my sister and nephew or my mom. My dad has since passed away, and our dinners aren't the same meals, but my sister, my mom, or I cook our best meals on Sunday for ourselves or for each other. If there's not a family gathering, I join friends for a meal at a favorite restaurant, or we go to a place we've never been to try something new.

Starting the week with worship helps me to put first things first. To keep God first makes my life better. The Sabbath is a symbolic reminder of that. I do my best to keep my shopping to a minimum, but I understand why restaurants are open. I enjoy not having to cook and being able to go out with friends on Sunday. Hospitals, law enforcers, emergency services, and transportation systems now have to run twenty-four hours in our modern world. Prayer, thanksgiving, praise, reading the Scriptures, communion, confession, and volunteering are all acts identified with the Sabbath. I can do those things on any day. It's great to come together, and we should do that, but the daily actions and faith in one's heart are more important than a day in and of itself.

—Brian Medoro
Television advertising account executive

24

family time

On weekends, the kids will sometimes have a "No-TV Day." On those days, we do not turn on the television. We play board games, play games outside, or the kids help with household chores—washing clothes, making beds, planting flowers. I find involving them in household chores early on gives them a sense of responsibility, and if you make it fun they won't give you a hard time when they get older. We take a lot of timeouts for horseplay and silly stuff. It will take longer to get your work done, but the kids really enjoy helping out.

—Dawna White
Wife of Bob/mother of Stephen and Brennen

Dawna shared her ideas with others in her community on how to use time to enrich the family unit. They came up with the following lists for you to try and hope you will add a few of your own.

Family Time

Indoor Activities	Outdoor Activities
Watch a black and white movie with grandparents and talk about how the world has changed.	Roller skate
	Ride bikes
Have a debate about current issues.	Play volleyball with neighbors
	Visit a historical site
Look at old photographs and write on the back who the people are.	Play hopscotch
	Go for a walk
Prepare a meal together.	Play catch
Exercise together.	
Write poems to each other.	
Play board games.	

—Used by permission of *Proud Neighbor Magazine*
www.proudneighbor.com

25

matthew 12:8

For the Son of man is Lord, even of the sabbath day.

26

sabbath hands

YOUNGER VIEW

I honestly like participating in my Sunday school class and learning about the Bible. I usually have a lot of homework during the week, so if I'm all caught up by Sunday afternoon that is my free time. I play on the computer for hours, watch television, and play with my dog and cat. There are kids at my school that go to Wednesday youth group meetings at their churches, but for some, Sunday is the only time they can go to church. I wouldn't mind if there were a law mandating Sunday as the day of rest. It would stop some people from being workaholics. Sunday is a reminder that we shouldn't worship things. If I had a car, I would never wash it instead of going to church. I would wash it when I got home.

—Danielle Edghill
High school student

Don't You Need Some Rest?

ELDER PERSPECTIVE

When I was a child, even if it we didn't have a lot of fancy food for Sunday dinner, there were always biscuits. I still make biscuits and piecrust from scratch. I've taught my granddaughter Danielle how to make them, and you should see how she holds a bowl and whips that dough. She's very good at it. It's nice I've been able to pass this Sunday tradition down to her. In my younger days, folks had to prepare for Sunday because you couldn't find a store open. It was a day to focus totally on God and give him honor.

—Lillian Williams
Danielle's grandmother

27

sabbatical year Defined

Sabbatical year: 1. A year in which land remained unseeded, observed every seven years by the ancient Jews. 2. A leave of absence with pay, usually granted every seventh year, as to a college professor, for travel, research, or rest. In this sense, also called "sabbatical leave." (*American Heritage Dictionary of the English Language*)

28

NANA'S HOUSE

My mother, brother, and I used to go to my grandmother's house on Saturday. I called her Nana. During one of our visits, it began to snow, and the storm grew so great we all had to spend the night. Nana's mom, my great-grandmother, was a big-time cook. The two elder women lived in the house with Nana's five sons. The house had a kitchen, breakfast room, and dining room. I recall how good it felt when I woke up that snowy Sunday and found that we were having breakfast in the dining room! We generally ate there only on special occasions. I still remember that biscuits and grits were on the menu. My mother never ate or cooked grits, so that was something new for me.

I was very close to my nana. I could get to her even when I couldn't be near my mother because nana was always home. That is, she was always home every day but Sunday. That snow day was an exception. She let it be known that Sunday was her day. She went to church and then to her girlfriend's house for dinner. You were only supposed to come and get her from North Penn Baptist Church or Miss Frances' house in case of an emergency. That was the one time during the week she had her girl talk and didn't do any work for anyone. I sometimes felt uneasy about that. We all went to the same church, and I always remembered how to get to Miss Frances' house—just in case.

As I grew older, Sunday after church was a lonely time for me. My mother worked at night so she had to sleep. I longed for company. My friend Glo was in a similar position, and whenever we could we'd take long walks into the evening and get back home in time to watch the *Ed Sullivan Show* on television.

My Sunday afternoons aren't boring anymore, and I realize God gave the Sabbath for rest from the beginning of time. It's needed for every age. For those who don't go to church, they still know church doors are open and that some take the day to worship together. Just seeing others go through that ritual can provoke divine thoughts. It draws people to God. Every weekend, all society is reminded we have choices.

—Bernadette Edghill
Danielle's mother

29

THE LAWN MOWER

When I was a child, it was considered a sin in my neighborhood to mow your lawn on Sunday. I remember sitting in church in the quiet of morning service and hearing the minister point out the sound of a distant lawn mower damning how Satan was at work in the community. I never paused to wonder if the mower might be of another faith and perhaps I had offended him yesterday by doing my early morning yard work. I wasn't even sure why it was a sin, but I was sure that passing out the punishments was God's department, so I put it from my mind. I came away with the idea that even if you weren't in church on Sunday morning, where, of course you were expected to be, you had better not go outside before noon.

Each week my family gathered around a large Sunday dinner at my grandmother's table. It took hours to prepare the food and clean up afterwards, but I never thought of that work putting her dear soul in danger. Later, we often set off on long car trips down dusty, country roads to visit family members and the sick that couldn't leave their homes. As I got older, I learned that travel and work on the Sabbath were forbidden in the Bible (Exodus 16:23), so it was never quite clear in my mind as to when God had changed the rules, or had he? After all, his instructions were to remember the Sabbath day; to keep it holy, restful, reflective, and quiet. That was a simple request. Had man's interpretation over the years added the confusion? Community traditions and Blue Laws* were intended as guidelines for accomplishing the greatest commandment of all—love for one another. If Grandmother was showing love by cooking for her family, or if visiting an elderly shut-in could bring joy, wasn't that God's intent? That answer can only be found in another's smile, a caring touch, a lifted spirit, and the reassurance that comes in quiet Sabbath moments when we can be still and listen.

Is it possible we're so busy telling God what we want that we don't take the time to listen to His reply? Jesus didn't mince words. The Sabbath was made for man, a time to rest in body and mind, a time to listen and focus. The "To Do" list never gets any shorter. While you are busy crossing off an item at the top, another item is being added at the bottom. Sometimes we just need time to evaluate where we are before we know how to move forward and why we're doing so.

Last Sunday morning I heard a neighbor crank a lawn mower, but instead of throwing stones in his direction I took him a glass of cold water. Sabbath begins in the heart.

—Sandy Roach
Electronics company sales representative

---

*Blue Laws: A body of laws that began in colonial England and brought to the United States designed to enforce certain moral standards and particularly prohibiting specified forms of entertainment, recreation, and business pursuits on Sunday.

30

Luke 6:9

Then Jesus said unto them, I will ask you one thing;
Is it lawful on the sabbath days to do good, or to do evil?
to save a life, or to destroy it?

31
Together

Even as a very young child, I loved good preaching and singing and everything that went along with the corporate worship experience. It was like theater to me the way people clapped and sang (often a cappella) in harmony. There was a bond of fellowship in a sanctuary filled with folks dressed in their best clothing testifying about the goodness of God despite whatever problems they'd experienced throughout the week. I didn't get that experience in class with my peers. So I preferred church over Sunday school, even though worship service was three times longer than the time I would have spent in youth sessions with children my own age.

I'm an only child. I always felt secure and happy sitting between my parents in church. I never ran off with other children. My mother was five feet tall and my dad stood just over six feet. He was considered tall in the community where we lived. His friends called him Big Mike and children called him Bear Mike—behind his back, of course. Seated between them, I knew I was protected, secure, and gently loved. That led me to understand my heavenly Father's love.

After church, while everyone was all dressed up in their Sunday clothes, my family would visit aunts, uncles, friends, or those in the hospital. When my mother, father, and I went to someone's house, they always served something special like hand-squeezed lemonade and/or homemade cake and ice cream. It seemed like everyone had been to church somewhere, so there was always a lot of discussion about the services and sermons. Good manners were expected of the other children and me. We had on our best attire and were expected to be on our best behavior.

Even though my family lived in the city, Sunday had a very laid-back feeling that some might call country. In the summertime, we watched baseball on television and ate watermelon. We often played board games like checkers and *Monopoly* or games like jacks that could be played on the porch or steps. During the cool seasons, my father baked pound cakes. He would jump on the kitchen floor while they were in the oven to make them fall so they would be heavy in the middle. He liked his cake like that, and they tasted delicious to me. We usually ate them warm right out the oven.

I still don't do housework on Sunday. It's a day to worship, rest, and relax. I cook, but I don't do much more than that. Everyone should have a day of rest to give his or her mind a chance to break its regular routine and renew itself. God commanded it. I pray and meditate everyday, but on Sunday, I prepare to worship with others by listening to gospel music and anthems.

I still have Sunday clothes, Sunday hats, and Sunday pocketbooks. They are kept separate until they get a little worn. Then they cross over into work clothes, and I shop for new church attire. It doesn't have to be expensive, but it's my best because I've deemed it special enough to set it aside for community worship.

Together

On Sunday mornings my dad would pour on the cologne. My mom and I used to say he really got "perfumed up" and that he wore enough for the three of us. Wherever our paths took us during the week, we always spent Sunday all together.

—Zella Michael
Child welfare social worker

32

Matthew 12:10-13

[10]And, behold, there was a man which had his hand withered. And they asked him, saying, Is it lawful to heal on the sabbath days? that they might accuse him. [11]And he said unto them, What man shall there be among you, that shall have one sheep, and if it fall into a pit on the sabbath day, will he not lay hold on it, and lift it out? [12]How much then is a man better than a sheep? Wherefore it is lawful to do well on the sabbath days. [13]Then saith he to the man, Stretch forth thine hand. And he stretched it forth; and it was restored whole, like as the other.

33

Just One Look

The ride to Sunday school always put me to sleep. Rumbles on the bridge woke me up and I knew we were five minutes from church. My father was superintendent of the Sunday school so I couldn't be late or misbehave. When I did clown around, he'd pop me up the side of my head. After class, my friends and I would run to the store and buy candy. We'd then go sit in the church balcony during worship service and try not to get caught acting up. Our parents were in the choir loft on the other side of the church but at our eye level. It's amazing how they could send one look across that sanctuary and whomever it was meant for would straighten up. After service, we'd go see the candy lady. Her name was Mrs. Trusty. Supposedly, she gave us candy if we'd been good, but she was a sweet old lady that loved children. We got a treat no matter how we acted.

If dinner wasn't being served at church, my father, mother, brother, and I would eat at Father Divine's* restaurant inside the Divine Lorraine Hotel. Everyone paid whatever they wanted to for meals. That's how the place was always run.

Don't You Need Some Rest?

I loved staying at church. If we didn't have an afternoon or evening service where we attended, we went to BTU (Baptist Training Union), afternoon or evening service somewhere else. You might think I would have stopped church hopping on Sunday when I became an adult because I had to go so much as a child, but I didn't. I especially loved afternoon communion service where there wasn't a pianist or organist. Every hymn was sung a cappella. That was some rich music. It wasn't until I got married and had a child that I cut back on the number of hours I spent in church on Sunday to do other family activities. Now things like birthday parties, the park, television, and tennis lessons take up most Sunday afternoons. My husband has a different attitude about what Sunday should be and I respect that. God is alive seven days a week and I don't have to box him into one day. It's easier for me to keep the family whole that way.

Only recently have I shopped at the market on Sunday morning. When I was a child, it didn't matter whether the mall was open on Sunday or not. I wasn't going. With so many faiths in society, some can take offense if one day is mandated over another like the Blue Laws tried to do. It's up to individuals and groups to honor the Sabbath. God commanded it so people would stop, look at what he's done, and honor him. When that happens, it helps us all. It fosters respect for our Creator and therefore respect for one another.

—Cynthia Malachi White
Human resources consultant

---

*Father Divine (1882?-1965) was an African American religious leader who preached the virtues of a disciplined, moral life, emphasizing communal living, racial equality, and celibacy. He established dozens of havens. The Divine Lorraine Hotel operated in Philadelphia, Pennsylvania until the late 1990s.

34

matthew 11:28

Jesus said, "Come unto me ye who that labour and are heavy laden, and I will give you rest."

35

no cussing

I always look forward to hearing the choirs and soloist sing on Sunday. The music always touches a place in my heart—a place deep in my heart—especially when the songs center on the minister's sermon. I listen to gospel music all day. Sunday is soul-food day, and I look forward to dinner whether I cook or eat at a restaurant. The Sabbath is a weekly reminder that hope and faith are the backbone of morals we all should and can live up to with the help of God. It's a replay of the message that when we mess up, grace lets us get up. I make an effort to be positive on the Sabbath Day—no cussing. It's a way to start the week knowing I can and should praise the Lord wherever I go.

—Karen Hill
Special education assistant

36

NO pressure

My sister and I were raised by a woman I would characterize in one word—*steady*. She studied and became a practical nurse and completed coursework at two Bible schools. She had rules, and we had to honor her house. She talked to us a lot, but she didn't put any pressure on us to adopt her beliefs. She had a personal Sunday mandate that she didn't watch television—not at all, not all day. By the time my husband and I became boarders in her home during the early years of our marriage and we were waiting for our house, that practice had not changed. After going to church, she would read and study. She never tried to keep us from television, but the house was so quiet on Sunday my husband and I usually opted to go out. We'd walk and talk about our plans for the future.

We've been in our own home for years now, but recently I've drifted back to our former landlady's practice. After church, I turn on the radio and listen to hymns and other services. I also catch up on all the reading I've put off during the week. Egypt in the Bible is often pictured as the place of bondage. There are certainly a lot of things that might not be bondage, but they certainly keep me busy all week. Even fun things on the weekend can leave me tired and unsatisfied when I don't pause to give God some quantity time. I recall the reminder of Deuteronomy 5:15: "And remember that thou wast a servant in the land of Egypt, and *that* the Lord thy God brought thee out thence through a mighty hand and by a stretched out arm: therefore the Lord thy God commandeth thee to keep the Sabbath day." Why would I pass up the chance to do that?

—Edna Hebron
Children's Bible club leader

37

No strangers

On a trip to Italy we were in Venice on a Friday. We decided to attend services in the old ghetto area of the city at a very traditional synagogue. Travelers, other visitors, and locals joined together as friends to pray, separated only by orthodox traditions—women on one side and men on the other. There was teaching and songs. Adults late for services chanted prayers in the corridor outside and children danced and played.

After service, we were swept along to a restaurant to share the Sabbath meal, guests of the owner and her rabbi husband. Hands were washed, the challah* blessed, and additional blessings said for the bountifulness of the table, family, and friends. When we commented on the generosity of our hosts, we were reminded that being together on the Sabbath was in itself a mitzvah (blessing) and that we were related by faith, regardless of the degree of our devotion.

When we took the water bus back to our hotel, we watched the group—many still dancing, singing, eating desserts, and joining together as friends and family in a foreign place, but united as one, sharing the common joy of observing the Sabbath.

As a child you wonder about the stranger among you. As an adult you realize there are no strangers. You are joined buy a common bond; chief among them is the celebration of the Sabbath. It is a declaration of faith and community. In joining together for prayer and enjoying each other's company afterwards, we know we always have something to share and that we are never alone.

—Sy and Sylvia Goldgehn
World travelers

---

*Challah: A loaf of yeast-leavened, white egg bread usually braided. It is traditionally eaten by Jews on the Sabbath, holidays, and ceremonial occasions.

38

Leviticus 25:6

And the Sabbath of the land shall be meat for you; for thee, and for thy servant, and for thy maid, and for thy hired servant, and for thy stranger that sourjourneth with thee.

39

Long Walks

There was something wonderful about a house full of the people I loved, all sound asleep on Sunday morning. I felt safe and vaguely naughty. I liked to softly walk about, just outside the bedrooms of my family members, listening to the gentle whistles of their slumber. We lived in a converted, old Victorian schoolhouse on a hill. The tall windows always stood with the curtains drawn back so the morning light came rushing in and woke me very early whether I wanted to or not. The light didn't bother anyone else. I usually had the house to myself for several hours.

I liked to go for long walks with our dog, Buck, as soon as I willed myself out of bed. I must have looked a little odd, walking beside the big wiry-haired, black and tan Airedale in my nightclothes, with my small feet bare and my hair standing about my head as wild as a mustang's tail.

Calvin and Hobbes was still a regular feature in the comics, and I lived all week for Calvin's Sunday wit. Sometimes I was early enough or the papergirl was late enough for the newspaper to still be warm. I loved the smell of it, and I loved the dusty feeling of the ink beneath my fingers as I toiled through the pages. I read it from front to back and read every single comic before I let myself even peek at *Calvin and Hobbes*. Buck always fell asleep at my feet, and when I invariably woke him up with my loud laughter, he would give me a long, reproachful look, indubitably conveying the opinion of his species everywhere that little girls should not laugh before 10 A.M. on Sunday morning.

Just as the first twinges of loneliness began to take their hold on me, my brothers would come down the stairs, joking with or socking each other as they wiped the crust of sleep from their eyes. My little sister loves to sleep and does so heavily. My mom used to rouse her just before we left for mass. She dressed hastily and ate her brunch in the car.

My mom liked to dress my sister and me in identical jumpers and shiny Mary Jane patent leather shoes. This I did not mind. She also insisted, however, on slicking back our hair into ponytails, various knobs, or crimps, and then splashing us down with enough hairspray to gag a fan. On top of this discomfort, our feet were bound in stylish anklet socks. A big fluffy rim of lacing ran round the tops of them and itched our skin like ants. The boys were stuffed into miniature blue suits. Their breathing was halted by bright red bow ties that probably felt like nooses.

With four boys and two girls for my parents to suds and starch, we were always late for church. My grandparents and a multitude of aunts, uncles, and their respective progeny could usually reserve us a row, so that we rarely had to stand. I can remember that we were made to spend some holidays, though, crumpled atop the radiator, behind another wall of people left without seats.

After church, we piled into the fleet of vehicles belonging to my family and bussed ourselves to Nana and Papa's house. It didn't matter much what car you rode in. The lot of us fought like cats and dogs to ride with Steve and Julie, the youngest adults, who let us clamber all over each other and hang out the windows. Amazingly, we always arrived intact. In the summer, we spilled out onto the lawn, loll-gagging in the pear trees and constructing in the sandbox until brunch, which was usually fried ham and egg sandwiches, bacon, hash brown potatoes, and fruit. On winter mornings, we waited in the sprawling playroom upstairs, immersed in our minute kingdoms of *Lego* men and various small plastic toys.

My nana and papa lived in a beautiful house they had built when the neighborhood was only a few houses long and when the golf course, running behind it, was young and unknown. It was a big brick house, full of nooks and crannies, and wonderfully landscaped. There were big rocks and bushes scattered all about and magnificent gardens full of blooms, bugs, and snakes. Dividing the lawn from the golf course was a big shining creek with minnows and frogs. It was lined with badly hit golf balls. We made good money selling them back to the golfers, alongside weeping cups of lemonade. Our customers were mostly old men with paunchy bellies, red noses, and small bright eyes radiating smile lines. They liked us, and we liked them. Sometimes they would come to my grandfather and us. He knew everybody.

When it was warm outside, we all visited until it was very late, all covered with the sticky Kansan film that clings to you during the summer season. I remember the Sundays of my youth, full of well, happy people clustered everywhere, laughing, and talking. Kids ran helter-skelter between the legs of bigger people, and dogs galloped behind them with their tongues leaping out their mouths.

As the evening came and families eased into exodus, we all moved around to the front yard, pulling up wicker chairs to sit in and say goodbye. After the first group left, the next hour or so there was a steady trickle of "see yous," and my family was always the last to leave. "Kiss Nana and Papa good night, now, children, and say thank you," the elders said. We bleated obediently in identical gratitude and kissed the proudly beaming cheeks of our forebears with sticky lips.

Long Walks

I have lived many good days, but it is on the Sabbath that I have lived and loved best.

—Paula Fulbright
Freelance writer

40

Hebrews 4:9

There remaineth therefore a rest to the people of God.

41

awe in the air

I was taught to prepare for Sunday on Saturday. My brothers, sisters, and I all had assignments. We shopped, cleaned house, washed, ironed, and cooked, because none of these things were to be done on Sunday. Saturday night, while we were finishing our chores, we would listen to the radio. Our special program was *The Hit Parade.* The top ten songs of the day were played.

Faiths that worshipped on Saturday would ring their bells at 12 noon and again at 6 P.M. This put a special atmosphere in the air. I didn't know a lot about what was in the Bible then, but the sound of the chimes gave me a sense of awe.

When the local Kroger Store closed on Friday, Mr. Kroger sat out behind the building whatever fish hadn't sold, and anyone who wanted it could have it. If my grandfather stopped by, we'd have fried fish with our weekly hot rolls for Sunday morning breakfast. My brothers, sisters, and I all loved to hear our father say grace. That weekly prayer was the time he verbally expressed his Christianity while we were all together. The Wings Over Jordan Choir was popular then, and we loved to hear them over the radio on Sunday morning. Their signature song, *There Must be a God Somewhere*, was our family's favorite.

During the day, we attended Sunday school, morning church service, BYPU (Baptist Youth Prayer Union) in the afternoon, and evening worship. Throughout the year, when the weather was not too cold, there were tent meetings, which was a good way to have church outside. No one had air conditioners then.

Throughout my life I've carried on most of the traditions of my youth, especially not shopping on Sunday. My husband and I ran a store for many years. He tried opening on Sundays for awhile, but that didn't last. It caused too much conflict between us. We all, including the children, were in there six days. That was enough.

We lived in a busy society. It was always busy, just not as high tech as today. So, the Sabbath is there. It's a gift from heaven for those of us who would like to be still and put aside the chores that have to be done to maintain life. We all need to be refilled for the next week. We mark other days for particular things: work, school, sports. It benefits everyone when individuals remember to set apart one day for worship, celebrating a mighty God. It's good to start the next seven days rested and with a divine focus. If more folks had that, perhaps we wouldn't have so much road rage and other negative things.

—Nannie Saunders Paige
Wife and mother

42

psalm 92
A song for the sabbath

[1]It is a good thing to give thanks unto the LORD, and to sing praises unto thy name, O most high: [2]To shew forth thy lovingkindness in the morning, and thy faithfulness every night, [3]Upon an instrument of ten strings, and upon the psaltery; upon the harp with a solemn sound. [4]For thou, LORD, hast made me glad through thy work: I will triumph in the works of thy hands. [5]O LORD, how great are thy works! and thy thoughts are very deep. [6]A brutish man knoweth not; neither doth a fool understand this. [7]When the wicked spring as the grass, and when all the workers of iniquity do flourish; it is that they shall be destroyed forever: [8]But thou, LORD, art most high for evermore. [9]For, lo, thine enemies, O LORD, for, lo, thine enemies shall perish; all the workers of iniquity shall be scattered. [10]But my horn shalt thou exalt like the horn of an unicorn: I shall be anointed with fresh oil. [11]Mine eye also shall see my desire on mine enemies, and mine ears shall hear my desire of the wicked that rise up against me. [12]The righteous shall flourish like the palm tree: he shall grow like a cedar in Lebanon. [13]Those that be planted in the house of the LORD shall flourish in the courts of our God. [14]They shall still bring forth fruit in old age; they shall be fat and flourishing; [15]To shew that the LORD is upright: he is my rock, and there is no unrighteousness in him.

43

center of attention

Next to the Lord, I recall children being the center of attention on Sunday. Sunday afternoon was the time church congregations held Tom Thumb weddings, piano recitals, and baby contests. It was a reason for people to gather and stay at church all day. Folks showed off their children. We were little stars with lots of self-esteem. These events were also fundraisers. My extended family lived in a three-story house where we paid thirty-three dollars each month in rent. Money was tight, so I can't imagine too much money was generated from the contests and programs, but that didn't matter. We children would be all dressed up. We'd be applauded and valued. We got to share God's special day with him. Those times helped me learn to value others and myself.

—Connie Jenkins
Spiritual sister mentor

---

*Thom Thumb weddings were pageants featuring children, staged as social events and fundraisers. They were reasons to get dressed up and go out.

44 Annual National Observance of Children's Sabbaths

Celebrated each October and endorsed by more than two hundred denominations and religious organizations, the National Observance of Children's Sabbaths unites tens of thousands of religious congregations of many faiths in speaking out and acting faithfully for justice for children and families. Created by the Children's Defense Fund, this event encourages a long-term commitment to help children and families through prayer, education, service, and advocacy.

During the Children's Sabbaths weekend, religious congregations hold special worship services, conduct religious education programs, and other congregational activities, inspiring people of faith to respond to children's needs and commit to making this a better and safer world for all children. Children's Sabbaths are held in individual congregations with many communities organizing interfaith services and activities. Planning guidance and other information is available at www.childrensdefensefund.org.

45

sunday sharing

On Sunday I get a chance to not only be reminded of God's love but to share and express that love. I do it in part by picking up children and taking them to Sunday school. I teach them that Jesus died on the cross for their sins and what is expected of them if they accept that and want to live the Christian life. Coming together with others on Sunday gives me chance to share in instruction with them on being Christlike and how to share my faith. It's a journey. Company is helpful and makes the travel more enjoyable and complete. God planned it that way.

—Michelle Venson
American and world history teacher

Sunday is about sharing. It's important for the saints of God to meet on a regular basis to worship Him and put all other things aside. Clubs, teams, and social groups do it. How much more important this must be for people of faith? A lot of people are really attached to their local churches, and I am too, but I also enjoy revivals with other congregations and hearing guest speakers. It's that sharing theme again—having communion to share in Jesus' suffering, corporate worship, and group singing. All those things are inspiring and encouraging. We can lead isolated lives at times. The Sabbath calls for a coming together. The stability of seeing God's people gathering each week is a reminder that while humans falter, God hasn't changed. Though society alters what is right and true, God is still here alive, well, and wanting to be the heart, not part, of his creation. I don't diminish the tragedy in our world, but there are still miracles and triumphant situations that only the knowing God can get the credit for. They start each Sunday with the sunrise on the first day of the week.

—Deborah Anderson
Community-based instruction assistant

46

sabbath old and new

The focus of the seventh day Sabbath was on rest. No work of any kind was to be done because it was pointing to the spiritual rest we have in Christ in that He did all the work required to save us. But the focus on the New Testament Sabbath is not on the cessation of physical labor: rather, the focus is on intense spiritual activity: worship, preaching, teaching the Word of God, fellowship, helping others, and sending the gospel into the world.

—Taken from Sunday The Sabbath?
Pamphlet published by Family Stations, Inc.

47

sabbath reflection

Perhaps the greatest hindrance to modern spirituality is the busy, hectic pace of today's society.

—Gregory R. Frizzell
Author of *Returning to Holiness*

48

psalm 37:7a

Rest in the LORD, and wait patiently for him.

49

COUSIN LOTTIE

I was the oldest grandchild in my family and spent a lot of time with my grandmother. On Sundays we would go to Golden Gate Baptist Church. I mostly remember the holiday plays, teas, and things like that. My religious instruction came during the weekdays. I attended Catholic school from elementary through high school. After church, my grandmother and I would go to Cousin Lottie's house. She had a big bosom. She could hold my cousin, Laura, and me at the same time. We loved to plop on and snuggle next to her. Laura and I had to be quiet when we first entered the house because there would always be rolls in the oven. If we made too much noise, they would fall. No matter when they were ready, we'd get a hot buttered roll right out of the oven.

I didn't attend church much as a teenager. I wanted to do things my own way. I've come to realize even the Lord had a day of rest and I am much less than He is. Now it's no struggle for me to go even though I seem to always get a run in my stocking or pop a button on Sunday morning. I try to cook or go out for a nice balanced meal and always eat my vegetables on Sunday. I particularly enjoy attending church services with friends and then going to a restaurant for dinner. It doesn't have to be anything big. Actually, I don't like a lot of hoopla on Sunday. I prefer to be quiet and reflect. Everyone should do that whatever his or her Sabbath is. Every day I am grateful, but on Sunday I'm particularly focused on giving thanks.

—Christina A. Crummey
Customer service representative

50

sabbath day's journey

S abbath Day's Journey: The distance a Jew could travel on the Sabbath without breaking the law was about 1,000 yards. The basis for the law was so that every person within a camp or city would be close enough to the center of worship to take part in the services without having to travel such a great distance that the Sabbath became a harried and busy day. *(Nelson's Illustrated Bible Dictionary, Thomas Nelson Publishers 1986)*

51

Big Meeting

Each year, from June through August, my sister, brother, and I would visit my grandmother in South Carolina. Ministers in the area where she lived had regular jobs in addition to their religious duties. They also traveled from one congregation to another. Worship service was held at my grandmother's church every second and fourth Sunday. That's when the minister was available to preach there.

The highlight of the summer was the Big Meeting, preceded by a week of revival. Today it would be called Homecoming. I always envied the older teenagers. They got to walk home on the highway after the revival each night. I was younger and had to ride in the car with adults.

There was plenty of food on Big Meeting Sunday. Every family took food that had been prepared Saturday or earlier in the week. My grandmother made coconut cake, lemon pie, chocolate cake, and sweet potato pie for dessert. She also fried chicken and baked a ham. She cooked for a living and was particular about what she ate and what we ate. Consequently, my siblings and I couldn't eat at the Big Meeting feast. We were always too busy playing to mind. We knew my grandmother always left food at home for our special company and us.

My grandmother was a widow, and Big Meeting weekend was the time each year Grandfather's brothers came to see her and us. Uncle Judson, Uncle George, and Uncle John always made an annual visit together. We felt a connection to our grandfather through them.

Back in the city, Sunday school was a must for anyone living under my mother's roof. She always cooked a fried-chicken Sunday dinner.

I still attend Sunday school. Christian education keeps me prepared for my work in the secular world. Sunday is also the day I lay out my clothes for the workweek—all five outfits ironed and hung on my bedroom door. If I didn't do that I'd never be on time Monday through Friday. I also enjoy a good game of football.

In the 1980s, I had Sunday hats (wide-brim, of course), shoes, purses, and suits that all matched. That meant a lot to me then. Today I don't have a separate wardrobe. I understand the thought that we should look our best for the Lord, but all those Sunday school lessons over the years have taught me that God is more concerned about what's in my heart than what I have on my body.

—Waunda Loadholt
Early childhood education specialist

52

isaiah 58:13-14

¹³If thou turn away thy foot from the sabbath, from doing thy pleasure on my holy day; and call the sabbath a delight, the holy of the LORD, honourable; and shalt honour him, not doing thine own ways, nor finding thine own pleasure, nor speaking thine own words: ¹⁴Then shalt thou delight thyself in the LORD; and I will cause thee to ride upon the high places of the earth, and feed thee with the heritage of Jacob thy father: for the mouth of the LORD hath spoken it.

join the sabbath conversation

Questions for individual reflection and book club or group discussion:

1. What are your favorite childhood memories, if any, of Sabbath traditions in your family and/or community?
2. What are your current religious or non-religious Sabbath traditions?
3. How can you adopt new Sabbath traditions or make your current ones more meaningful?
4. How do your Sabbath traditions enhance your life and work, or how might they enhance your life and work?
5. Living in such a diverse world, do you feel the concept of Sabbath benefit's today's society? If so, how?
6. What does it mean to you to "remember the Sabbath to keep it holy"?
7. Discuss implications of viewing Sabbath as a divine gift versus a ritualistic duty.

Use page at the end of the book to record your answers and begin your own Sabbath journal.

Do You Have a Sabbath Story?

Send experiences, thoughts, or memories you'd like to share in future essay collections to info@susiepaige.com.

Susie is available for speaking engagements and to lead Sabbath discussion groups and workshops. Contact her at:

410A Glen Echo Road
Philadelphia PA 19119
215-264-4460
www.susiepaige.com

Books make great gifts.

For copies of *Don't You Need Some Rest? 52 Sabbath Reflections for Stressful Living* order

by phone
1-877-421-READ (7323)

by mail:
Pleasant Word Order
PO Box 428
Enumclaw,WA 98022

online:
www.pleasantwordbooks.com

Price: $10.99 plus shipping and handling.

your sabbath journal

The Sabbath was made for man; and not man for the Sabbath. (Mark 2:27)

The Sabbath was made for man; and not man for the Sabbath. (Mark 2:27)

The Sabbath was made for man; and not man for the Sabbath. (Mark 2:27)

The Sabbath was made for man; and not man for the Sabbath. (Mark 2:27)

The Sabbath was made for man; and not man for the Sabbath. (Mark 2:27)

The Sabbath was made for man; and not man for the Sabbath. (Mark 2:27)

The Sabbath was made for man; and not man for the Sabbath. (Mark 2:27)

The Sabbath was made for man; and not man for the Sabbath. (Mark 2:27)

The Sabbath was made for man; and not man for the Sabbath. (Mark 2:27)

The Sabbath was made for man; and not man for the Sabbath. (Mark 2:27)

The Sabbath was made for man; and not man for the Sabbath. (Mark 2:27)

The Sabbath was made for man; and not man for the Sabbath. (Mark 2:27)

The Sabbath was made for man; and not man for the Sabbath. (Mark 2:27)

The Sabbath was made for man; and not man for the Sabbath. (Mark 2:27)

The Sabbath was made for man; and not man for the Sabbath. (Mark 2:27)

The Sabbath was made for man; and not man for the Sabbath. (Mark 2:27)

To order additional copies of

Have your credit card ready and call:

1-877-421-READ (7323)

or please visit our web site at
www.pleasantword.com

Also available at:
www.amazon.com
and
www.barnesandnoble.com

Printed in the United States
57697LVS00001B/121-180